Pebble® Plus

## Dogs, Dogs, Dogs

# All about Yorkshire Terriers

by Erika L. Shores

Consulting Editor: Gail Saunders-Smith, PhD

CAPSTONE PRESS
a capstone imprint

Pebble Plus is published by Capstone Press,
1710 Roe Crest Drive, North Mankato, Minnesota 56003.
www.capstonepub.com

*Library of Congress Cataloging-in-Publication Data*
Shores, Erika L., 1976–
All about yorkshire terriers / by Erika L. Shores.
p. cm.—(Pebble plus. Dogs, dogs, dogs)
Includes bibliographical references and index.
Summary: "Full-color photographs and simple text provide a brief introduction to Yorkshire terriers"—Provided by
publisher.
ISBN 978-1-4296-8729-4 (library binding)
ISBN 978-1-62065-297-8 (ebook PDF)
1. Yorkshire terrier—Juvenile literature. I. Title.
SF429.Y6S46 2013
636.76—dc23
                                                                              2011049824

**Editorial Credits**
Veronica Correia, designer; Marcie Spence, media researcher; Kathy McColley, production specialist

**Photo Credits**
Alamy: blickwinkel, 7; Fiona Green: 3, 5, 9, 13, 17; iStockphoto: ruthrose, 19, zilva, 21;
Shutterstock: Liliya Kulianionak, 11, SergiyN, cover, Vicente Barcelo Varona, 1, 15

## Note to Parents and Teachers

The Dogs, Dogs, Dogs series supports national science standards related to life science.
This book describes and illustrates Yorkshire terriers. The images support early readers in
understanding the text. The repetition of words and phrases helps early readers learn new
words. This book also introduces early readers to subject-specific vocabulary words, which are
defined in the Glossary section. Early readers may need assistance to read some words and to
use the Table of Contents, Glossary, Read More, Internet Sites, and Index sections of the book.

Printed in the United States of America in North Mankato, Minnesota.
122016    010174R

# Table of Contents

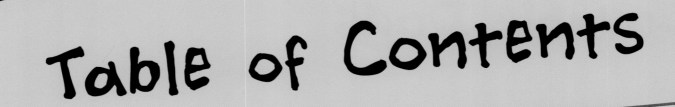

# Lovable Dogs

The small, friendly Yorkshire terrier first came from Yorkshire, England. People call these dogs Yorkies.

Long ago, Yorkies hunted rats.

Today Yorkies are still brave.

But they are more likely to sit

on their owners' laps

than chase rats.

# The Yorkie Look

Yorkies are the smallest

of all terrier breeds.

A Yorkie weighs between

4 and 7 pounds

(1.8 and 3.2 kilograms).

Yorkies grow shiny, silky hair.

The hair color on a Yorkie's back
and tail is called steel blue.

Its head, chest, and legs are tan.

Yorkies have small heads
and dark eyes.
Their ears are V-shaped
and stand straight up.

# Puppy Time

A newborn Yorkie is only
as big as a mouse.
Yorkie puppies have short,
frizzy hair. They grow quickly.
Yorkies live for 13 to 15 years.

# Doggie Duties

Owners care for their dogs every day. Yorkies should be fed a small amount of food two or three times a day.

Owners also brush

their Yorkies every day.

A topknot or a bow keeps

long hair out of a Yorkie's face.

# A City Pet

Yorkies are popular pets for people living in apartments or big cities. Their small size means they don't need large spaces for running and playing.

# Glossary

**brave**—having courage

**breed**—a certain kind of animal within an animal group

**popular**—liked or enjoyed by many people

**silky**—very soft and smooth like silk

**steel blue**—a very dark blue or black color

**terrier**—any of several breeds of small, lively dogs that were first bred for hunting small animals that live in burrows

**topknot**—the hair on a dog's head that is tied back with a small rubber band

# Read More

**Beal, Abigail.** *I Love My Yorkshire Terrier.* Top Dogs. New York: PowerKids Press, 2011.

**Green, Sara.** *Yorkshire Terriers.* Dog Breeds. Minneapolis: Bellwether Media, 2009.

**Hutmacher, Kimberly M.** *I Want a Dog.* I Want a Pet. Mankato, Minn.: Capstone Press, 2012.

# Internet Sites

FactHound offers a safe, fun way to find Internet sites related to this book. All of the sites on FactHound have been researched by our staff.

Here's all you do:

Visit *www.facthound.com*

Type in this code: 9781429687294

Check out projects, games and lots more at
**www.capstonekids.com**

# Index

Word Count: 192
Grade: 1
Early-Intervention Level: 15